ANCIENT CHINA FOR KIDS

Early Dynasties, Civilization and History
Ancient History for Kids
6th Grade Social Studies

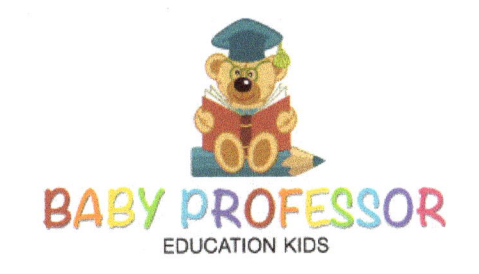

BABY PROFESSOR
EDUCATION KIDS

Speedy Publishing LLC

40 E. Main St. #1156

Newark, DE 19711

www.speedypublishing.com

Copyright 2018

All Rights reserved. No part of this book may be reproduced or used in any way or form or by any means whether electronic or mechanical, this means that you cannot record or photocopy any material ideas or tips that are provided in this book.

In this book, we're going to talk about the ancient civilizations of China. So, let's get right to it!

People have been living in what is now the country of China for thousands of years. During much of its recorded history, China was governed by various dynasties.

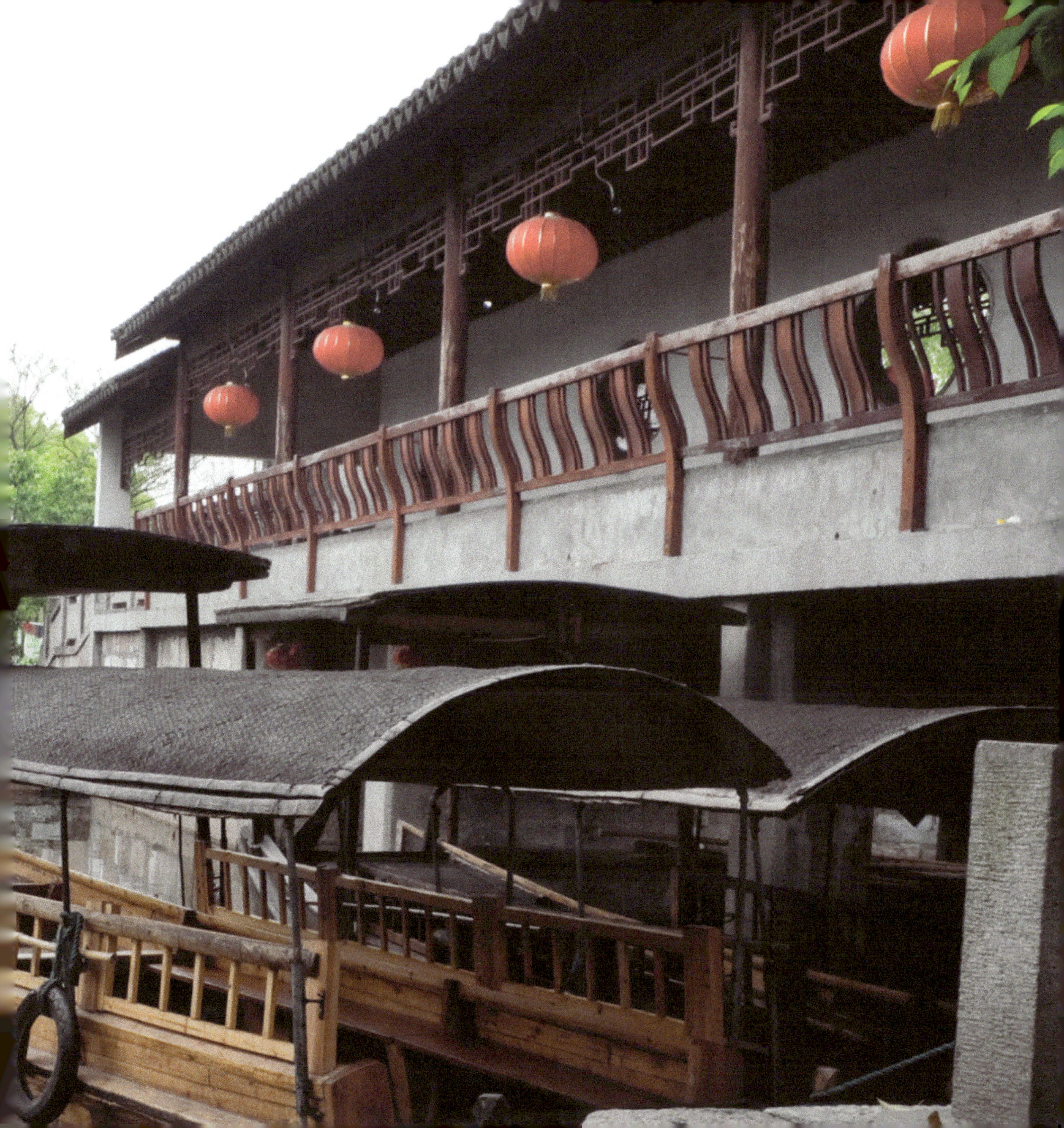

YANGDI CHINESE EMPERORS

WHAT IS A DYNASTY?

A dynasty passes the rule of the country from the father to the son. The ruler is generally called a king or emperor. When he passes away, more than likely the eldest son will take the throne or another close relative if there isn't an eldest son. A new dynasty begins when another family takes over.

WHAT WAS HEAVEN'S MANDATE?

The people of China believed that their gods had blessed their emperors and given them the power to rule. They called this right "Heaven's Mandate." In order to keep the favor of the gods, their rulers had to be honest and fair.

CHINESE EMPEROR

STATUE OF GUANYIM,CHINESE GOD

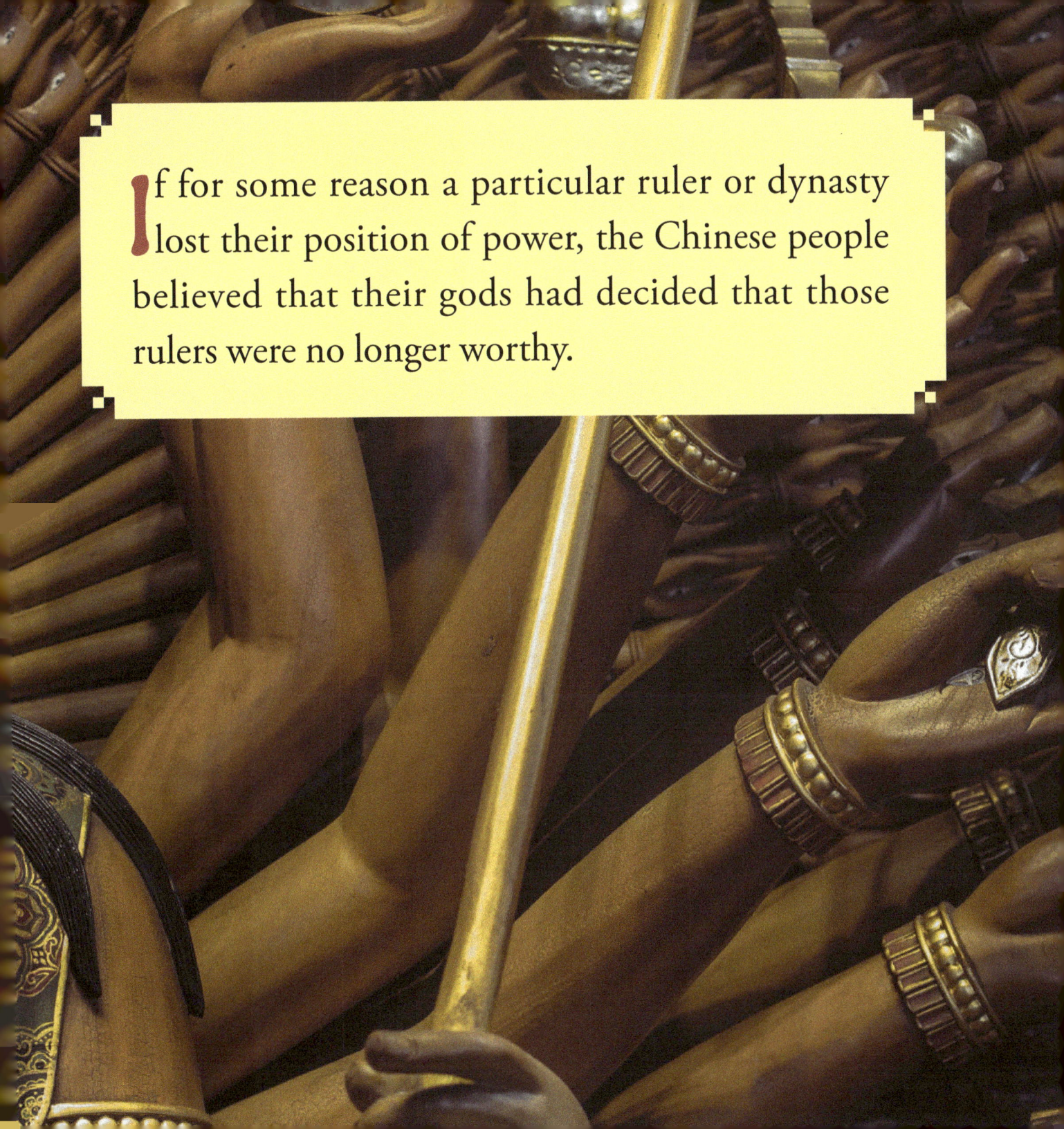

If for some reason a particular ruler or dynasty lost their position of power, the Chinese people believed that their gods had decided that those rulers were no longer worthy.

THE FIRST DYNASTIES OF ANCIENT CHINA

The following information provides summaries of the major periods of the first dynasties of ancient China. There is some overlap in the dates as dynasties transitioned from one to another.

GENERAL SHI LANG

OLD CHINESE COURTYARD HOUSE
(PINGYAO – SHANXI PROVINCE)

THE XIA DYNASTY
2100 BCE TO 1600 BCE

The Xia Dynasty is considered to be the first dynasty of ancient China. However, historians don't agree as to whether this dynasty actually existed or whether it is simply mythology or legend.

The dynasty's history is recorded in ancient Chinese texts, but archaeologists haven't found proof to substantiate these writings. If we assume that the Xia Dynasty existed, then it was the first because prior to that time, the king or emperor did not inherit the throne, but was selected based on talent and ability to rule.

損防一
尋防未
人萊莫
財

禹　克勤于邦　烝民乃粒
應數在躬　廓中允執
惡酒好言　九功由立
不伐不矜　振古莫及

YU THE GREAT

Yu the Great was the ruler who established the Xia Dynasty. He took the throne and acquired fame by constructing canals to control the Yellow River's floods.

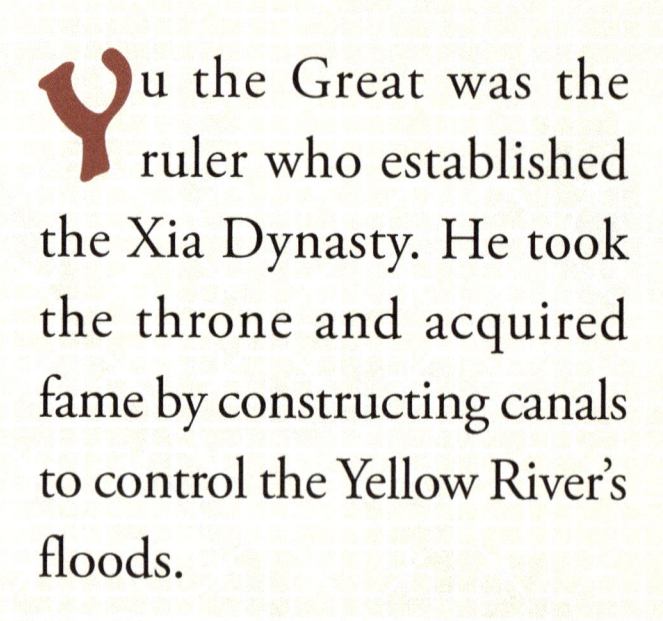

He was king for forty-five years. After Yu passed away, his son took the throne. His name was Qi and his rule was the beginning of a span of five centuries where his family's descendants ruled.

QI

Throughout this long dynasty, there were seventeen different rulers. Some of these rulers were fair and ruled with wisdom, such as the first ruler, Yu the Great, as well as Bu Jiang, who ruled for the longest period and was considered very wise.

EMPEROR QIN SHI HUANG

ANCIENT CHINESE SPEARS AND SCULPTURE OF TERRACOTTA SOLDIERS ON GREAT WALL(CHINA)

Others were very cruel. King Jie was the last king of the Xia Dynasty. He was an evil tyrant and he was eventually removed from his position. Then, the Shang Dynasty began.

ANCIENT PROVINCE OF CHINA

During the Xia Dynasty, Yu the Great organized the lands of China into nine separate regions that were called provinces.

CHINESE VILLAGE ON THE RICE TERRACE

These provinces were ruled by feudal lords who pledged their loyalty to Yu. At this point in time, China was a farming culture.

CASTING BRONZE

The people had learned how to caste bronze, but their tools were still simple implements made of stone and pieces of bone. They made advances in agriculture, including the practice of irrigation. They also created a type of calendar.

THE SHANG DYNASTY 1600 BCE TO 1046 BCE

Because the Shang Dynasty was the first dynasty with written documentation, some historians believe it was the first of the Chinese dynasties. Others think it was after the Xia Dynasty. The tribe of people called the Shang became powerful enough under the leadership of Cheng Tang to overthrow the evil King Jie.

PUNISHMENT OF THE BASTINADO

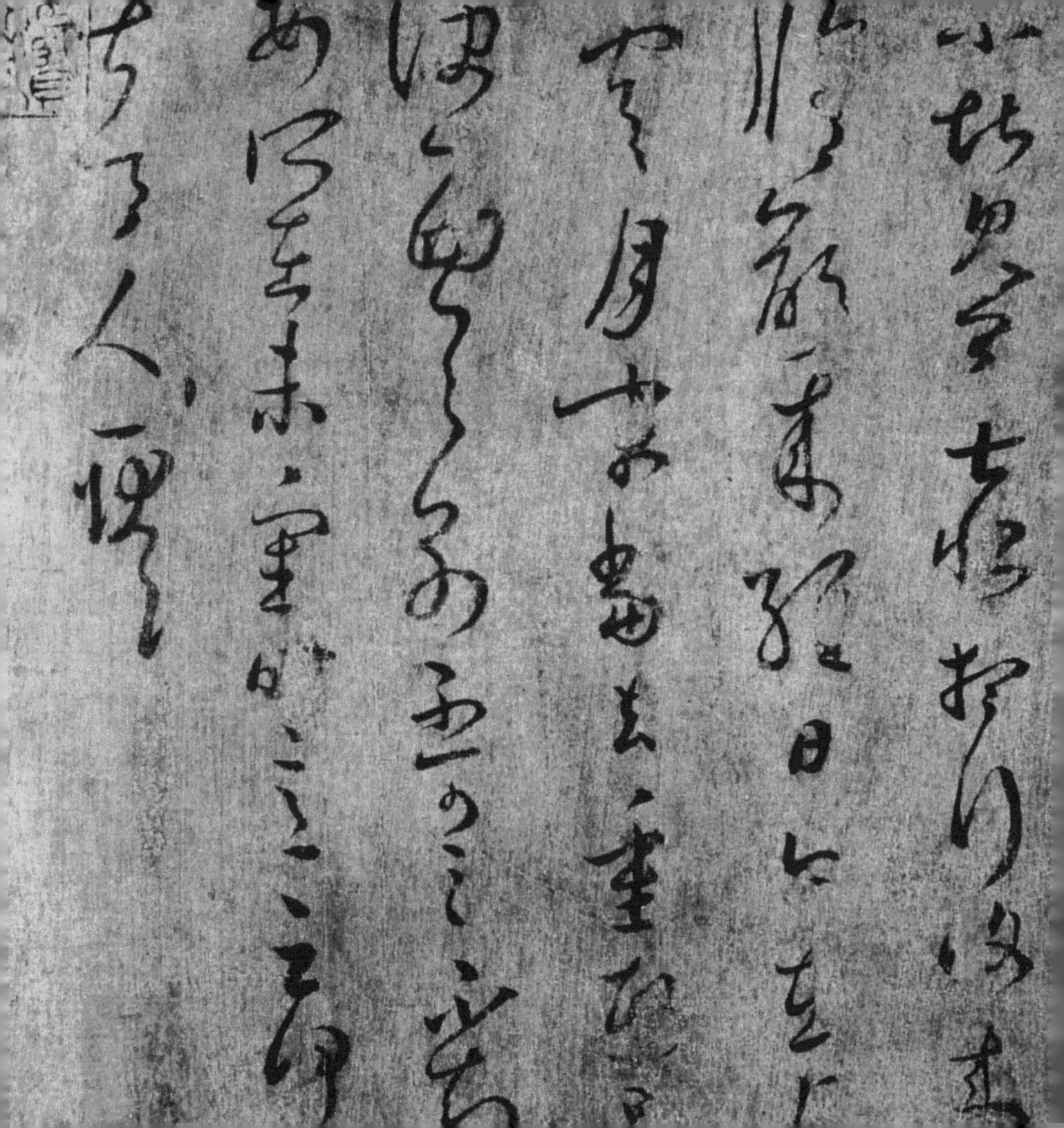

亂得人心懷
怕ら不至未畫其之三名
怕々迴之盡其三之岂
雲月せ畫去重叹
悵觀喜日と至
小姑罗志帚り没き

The history of the Shang Dynasty was written during later dynasties and archaeologists have found thousands of bones used to foretell the future. The inscriptions on these bones give a great deal of insight into the culture and history of the Shang. Because the Shang were the first to invent a form of writing, which was similar to modern Chinese writing, their government was well-organized and advanced.

During the Shang Dynasty there were innovations in the manufacture of bronze, which was used for religious artifacts and weapons. Bronze weapons gave them an advantage as they fought against their enemies.

TWO BRONZE KNIVES – SHANG DYNASTY

ZHOU DYNASTY CARRIAGES

THE ZHOU DYNASTY 1046 BCE TO 256 BCE

The Zhou Dynasty ruled China longer than any other dynasty. One of the Shang Dynasty's states was Zhou. A leader by the name of Wen Wang created a plan to take over the Shang Dynasty. After years of strategizing, Wen's son Wu began an uprising and led soldiers as they crossed over the Yellow River. They overthrew the Shang.

The Zhou leaders proclaimed that the Shang leaders had become corrupt. To secure their position they introduced "Heaven's Mandate."

ANCIENT TEMPLE IN HONOR OF ANCESTORS

The Zhou Dynasty operated by dividing their lands into regions called fiefs. These fiefs were ruled by the emperor's relatives. They owned the land as well as the farmers who toiled there.

The last part of the Zhou Dynasty is known for two famous religions that developed at that time—Taoism and Confucianism. In addition to these new religions, there were also innovations in technology.

TAOIST TEMPLE GUANGZHOU GUANGDONG, CHINA

The Chinese people learned to create stronger tools and weapons from cast iron. In agriculture, they created the process of crop rotation.

Starting around 475 BCE and lasting until the end of the Zhou period, there were only seven states remaining within the Chinese empire. They were constantly at war with each other. The powerful and ambitious leader of the Qin region, named Qin Shi Huang, overthrew the other states. He declared himself emperor of a united country.

QIN SHI HUANG

QIN SHI HUANG IMPERIAL TOUR

THE QIN DYNASTY
221 BCE TO 206 BCE

Qin Shi Huang wanted his empire to last forever so he started many reforms to organize the newly unified country. He sectioned the country into 36 administrative regions called "commanderies" and made it known that any new government officials would be appointed based on their talents and knowledge.

ANCIENT CHINESE COINS

He established a common form of money to be used throughout the empire as well as a standard system of measurements. These innovations helped the unified country to gain a more efficient economy.

Another reform took place in the area of writing. Throughout China, there were many different forms of writing that were being used. The emperor mandated a specific type of writing to be taught and used throughout the empire.

In addition to these changes, Emperor Qin began many ambitious building projects. He added interconnecting roads as well as canals that quickly improved traveling and trading throughout the land. He also established the construction of what is now called the "Great Wall." His goal was to create a barrier so that tribes from the north couldn't travel south and invade China.

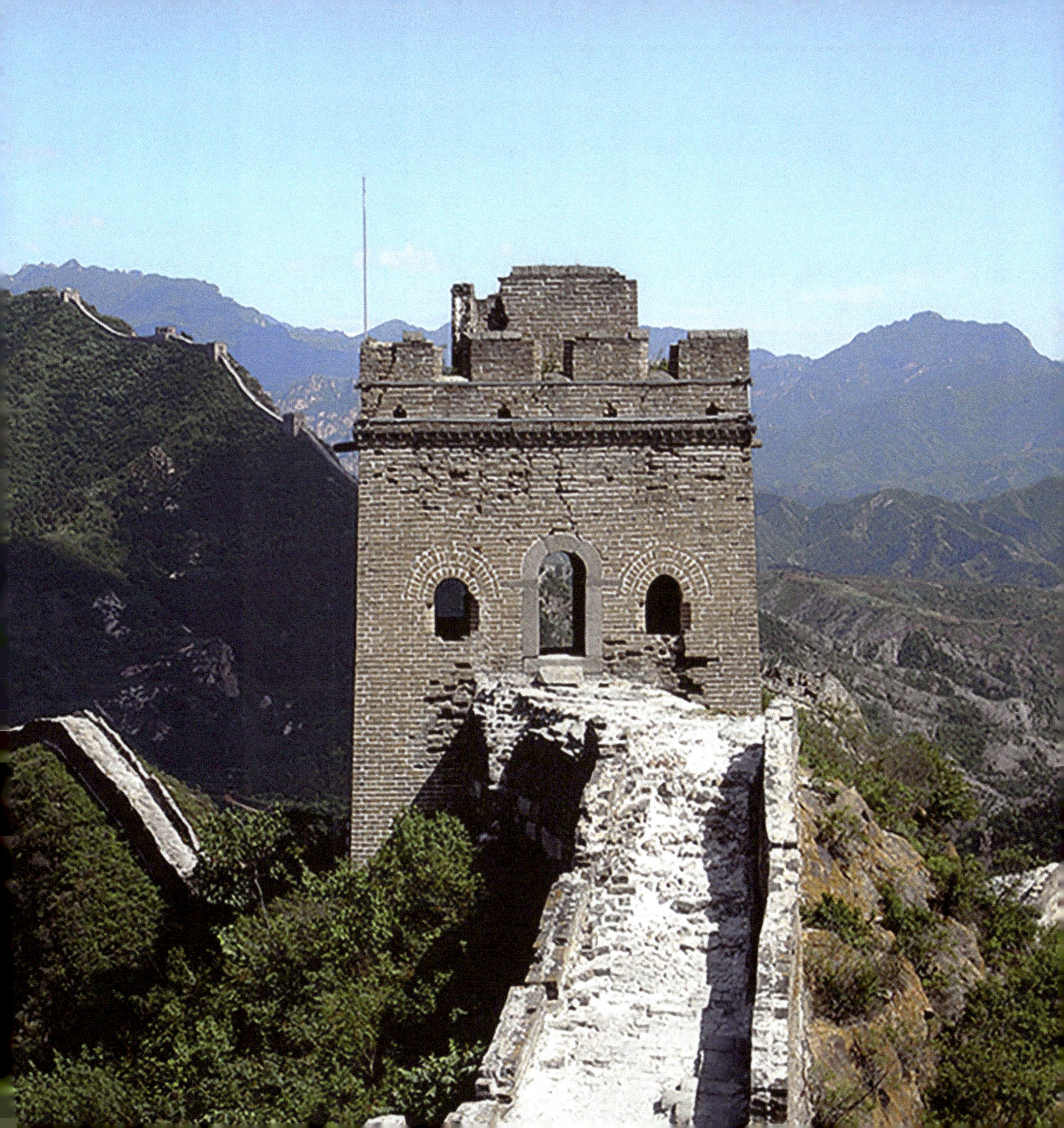

Qin was a masterful leader, but he was also tyrannical. He mandated the end of most forms of religion and ordered the burning of books so he could rewrite history and put himself and his empire first in China's history. He also became obsessed with living forever. He had the best scientists in China working on an immortality potion for him. Ironically, some of the potions contained liquid mercury, which is a potent poison and is probably what killed him.

QIN SHI HUANG 18TH CENTURY

At the same time that he was trying to find a way to avoid death, the emperor had a gigantic tomb with a terracotta army built.

STATUE OF EMPEROR QIN SHI HUANG NEAR THE SITE OF HIS TOMB IN XI AN, CHINA

QIN DYNASTY SOLDIERS FROM THE TERRACOTTA ARMY OF QIN SHI HUANG'S MAUSOLEUM

In case he passed over into the afterlife, he could be a great conqueror once again with the help of these terracotta soldiers.

ORNAMENTAL GATEWAY (PAILOU) FROM HAN DYNASTY

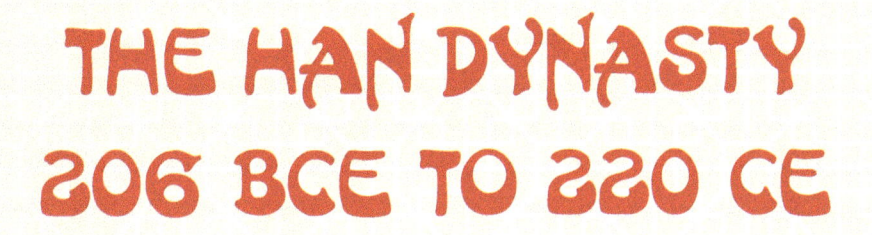

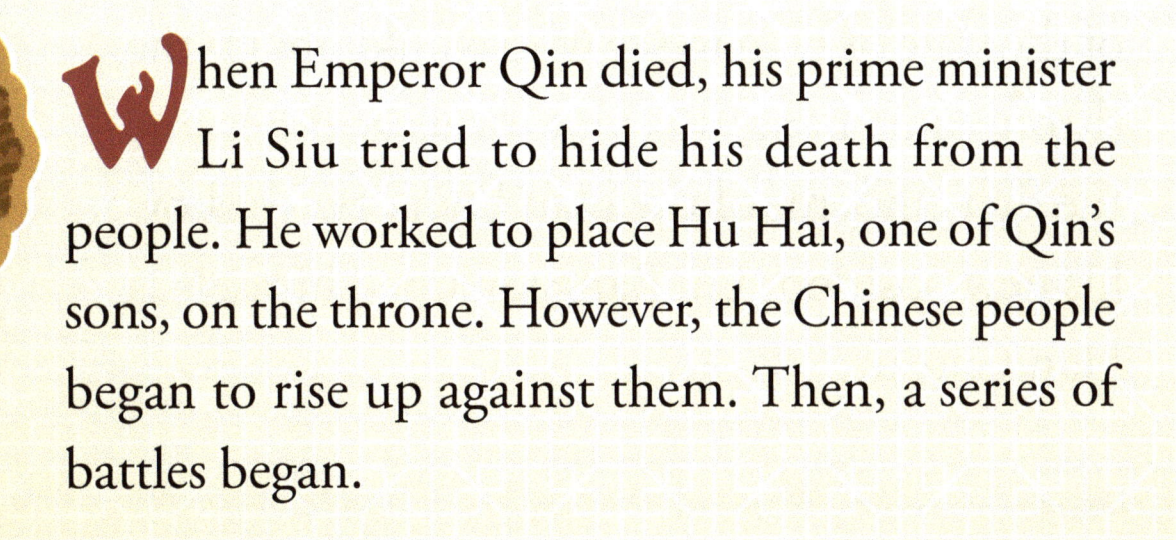

THE HAN DYNASTY
206 BCE TO 220 CE

When Emperor Qin died, his prime minister Li Siu tried to hide his death from the people. He worked to place Hu Hai, one of Qin's sons, on the throne. However, the Chinese people began to rise up against them. Then, a series of battles began.

The leader of the state of Chu, who was named Xiang-Yu, fought against Liu Bang of the state of Han to see who would obtain the throne. Liu Bang was victorious and became the first emperor of the Han Dynasty. To show his new position, Liu Bang renamed himself as Han Gaozu.

武皇帝劉秀

HAN GAOZU

Emperor Gaozu began a new form of government. He started a civil service and gathered the most intelligent citizens to hold these positions. Later emperors began schools with civil service examinations to ensure that only the best and brightest would obtain these jobs. Gaozu's innovations remained a part of the structure of the government for the next two thousand years.

SUMMARY

For a large portion of China's ancient history, dynasties ruled the empire. In a dynasty, power is transferred from one family member to another, typically from the father to the eldest son. Chinese legend states that the Xia Dynasty was the first. Today, many historians believe that the Xia Dynasty only exists in legends since there is no archaeological evidence. Beginning with the Shang Dynasty, there were written records, so historians have more details about the lives of people in ancient China from that point on.

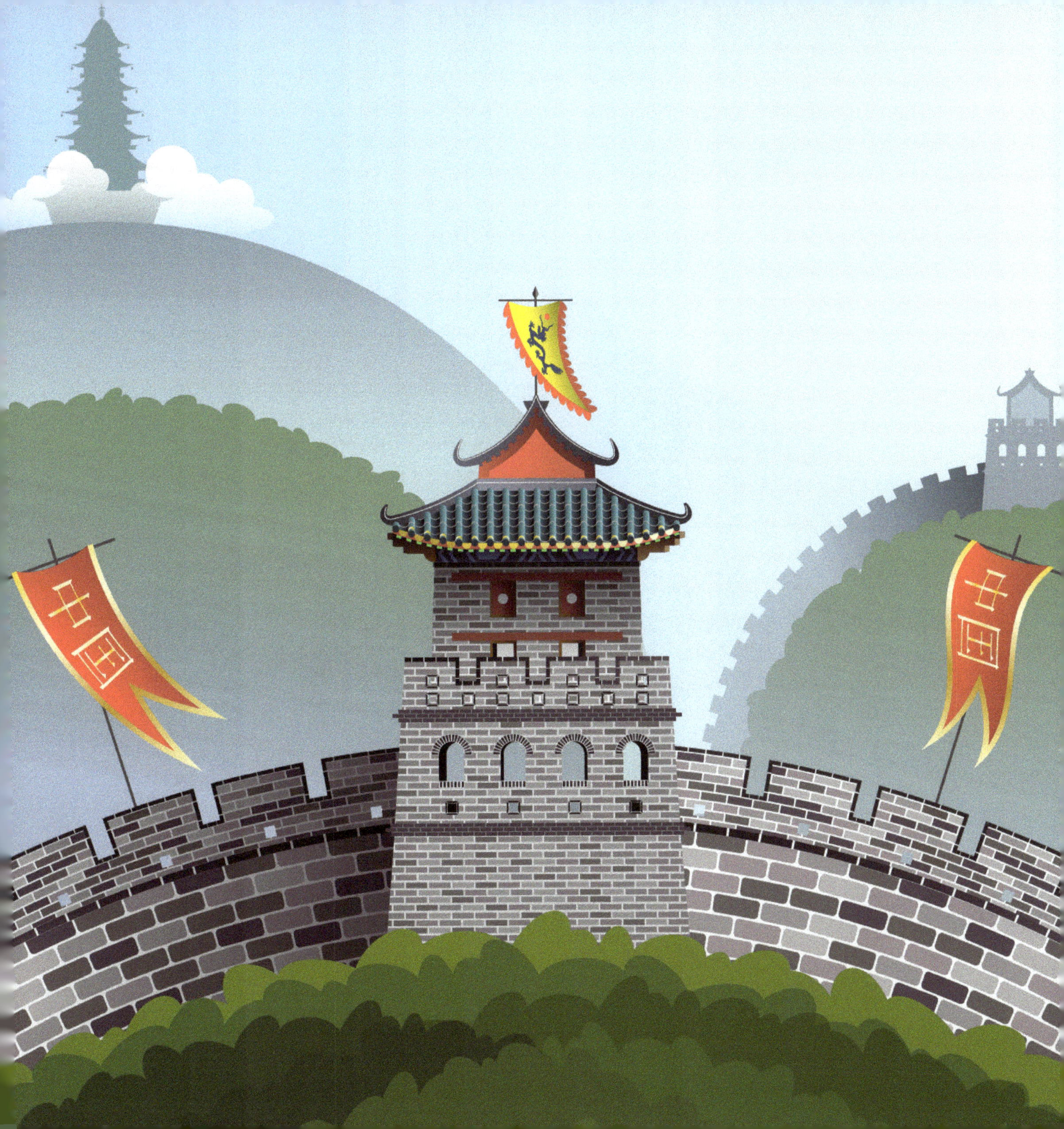
中国
中国

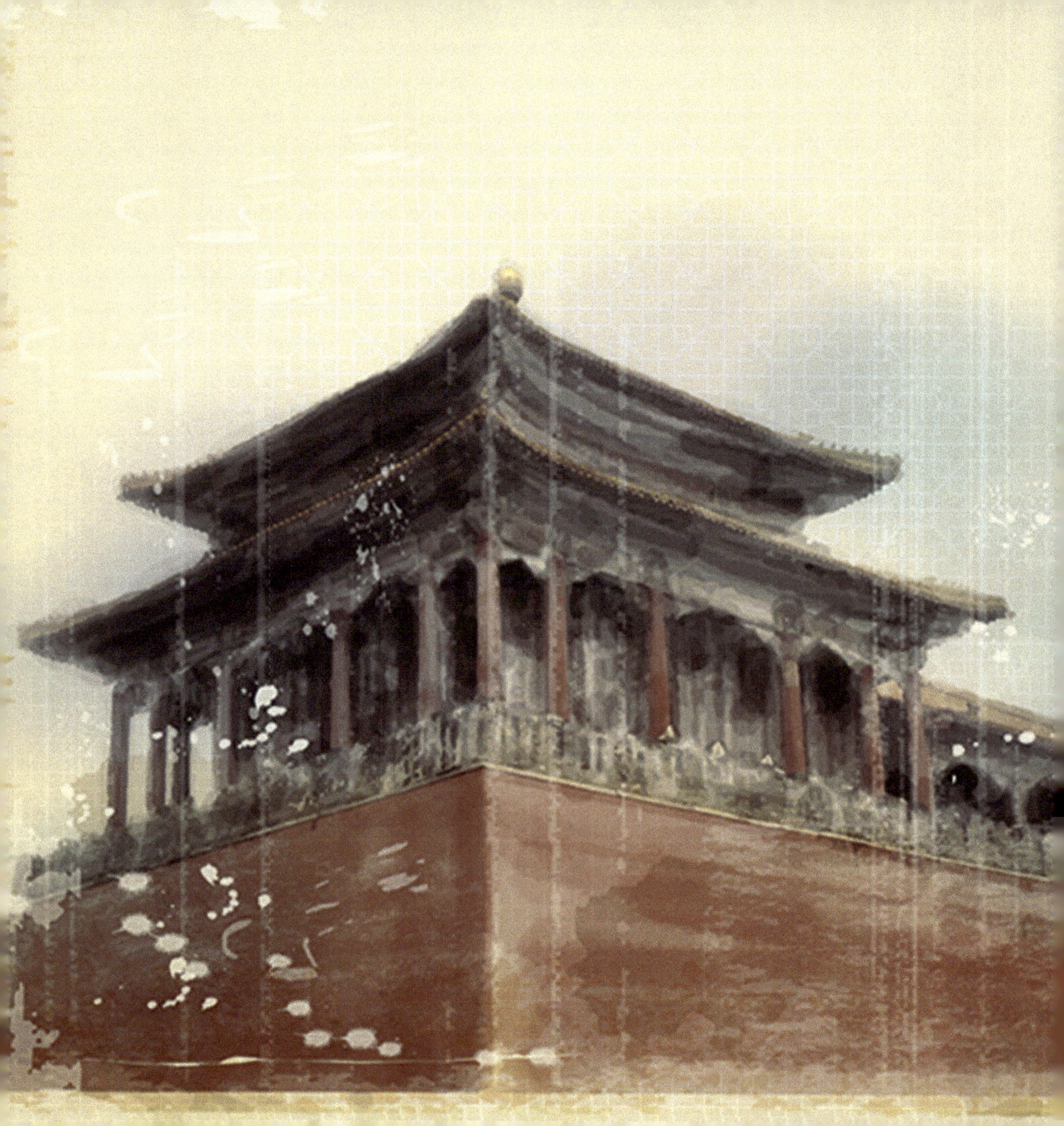

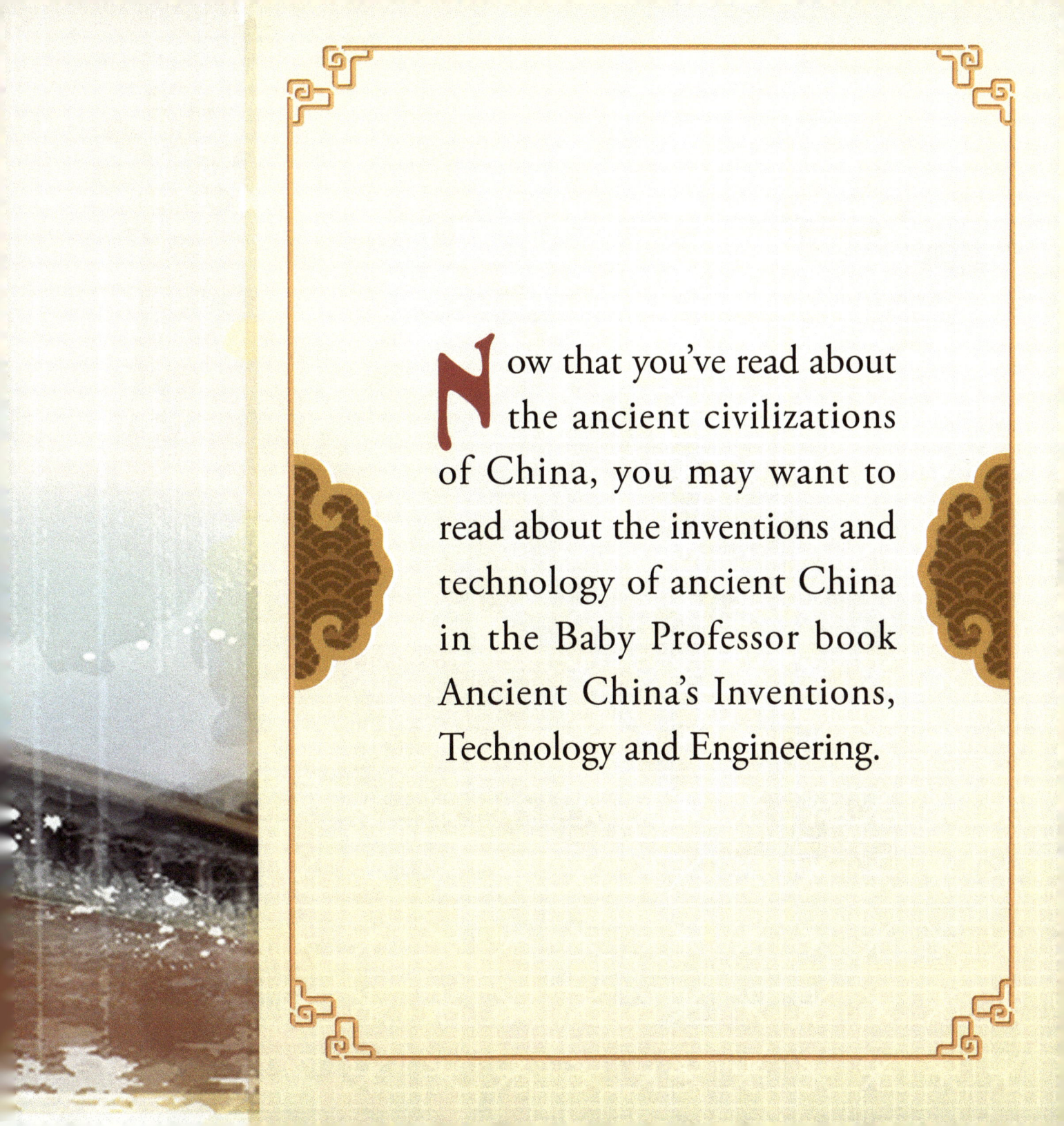

Now that you've read about the ancient civilizations of China, you may want to read about the inventions and technology of ancient China in the Baby Professor book Ancient China's Inventions, Technology and Engineering.

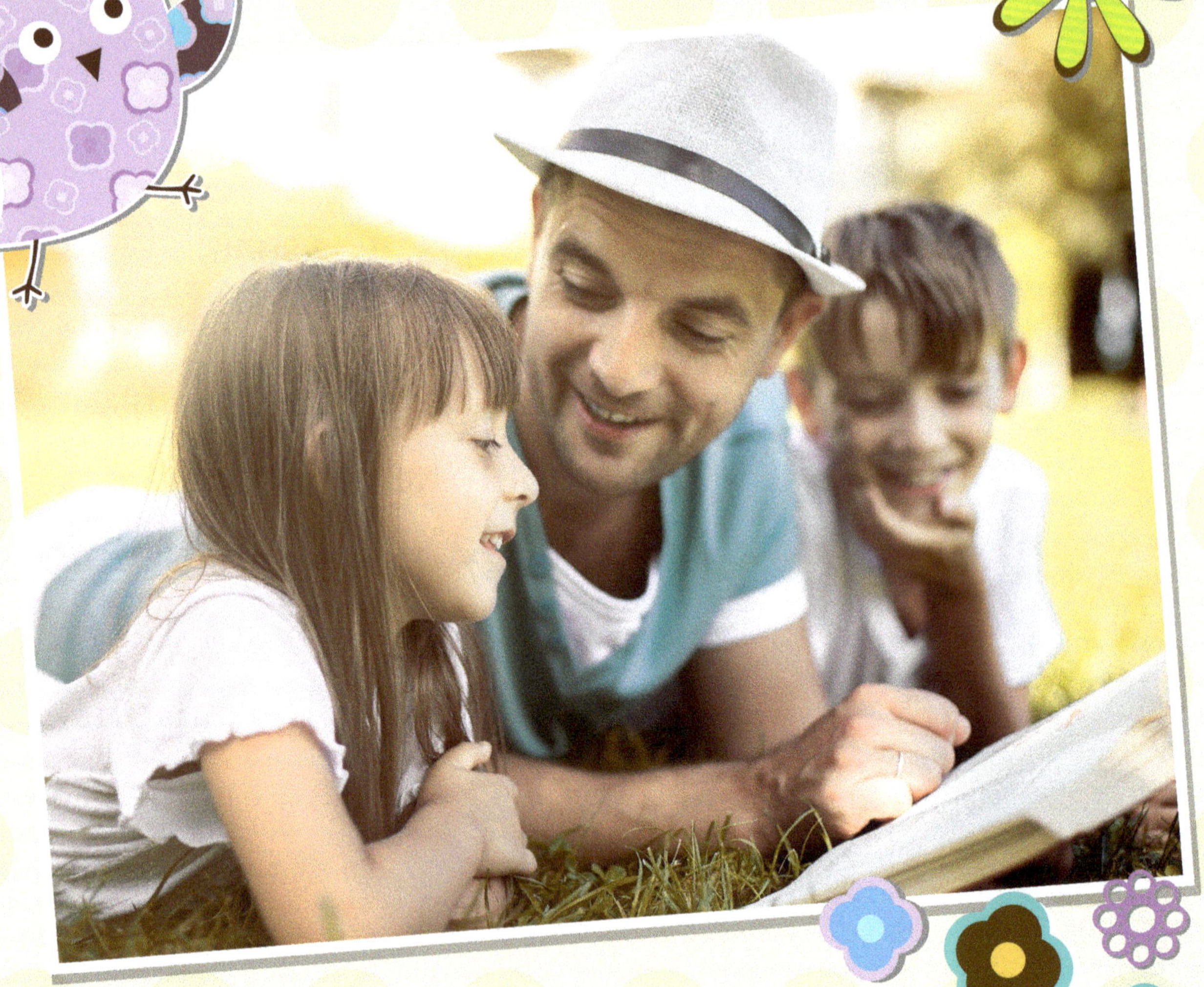

Visit

BABY PROFESSOR
EDUCATION KIDS

www.BabyProfessorBooks.com

to download Free Baby Professor eBooks
and view our catalog of new and exciting
Children's Books